SPOTLIGHT ON WEATHER AND NATURAL DISASTERS

METEOROLOGY AND FORECASTING THE WEATHER

GERALDINE LYMAN

PowerKiDS press™

NEW YORK

Published in 2019 by The Rosen Publishing Group, Inc.
29 East 21st Street, New York, NY 10010

Editor: Elizabeth Krajnik
Cover Design: Michael Flynn
Interior Layout: Rachel Rising

Photo Credits: Cover The Washington Post/Getty Images; Cover, pp. 3, 4, 5, 6, 8, 10, 12, 13, 14, 16, 17, 18, 20, 21, 22, 23, 24 (background) chaowat kawera/Shutterstock.com; p. 4 Alexey Lesik/Shutterstock.com; p. 5 dolphfyn/Shutterstock.com; p. 7 https://commons.wikimedia.org/wiki/File:Evangelista_Torricelli_-_Museo_di_Storia_Naturale_di_Firenze.JPG; p. 7 (inset) Courtesy of Library of Congress; p. 9 Pacific Press/LightRocket/Getty Images; p. 11 Kim Steele/Photodisc/Getty Images; p. 12 Courtesy of NOAA Libary; p. 13 Mike Focus/Shutterstock.com; p. 15 Martin Minnis/EyeEm/Getty Images; p. 16 Ryan McGinnis/Moment/Getty Images; p. 17 MonoLiza/Shutterstock.com; p. 19 Fox Photos/Hulton Archive/Getty Images; p. 20 2p2play/Shutterstock.com; p. 21 simonkr/E+/Getty Images; p. 22 oliveromg/Shutterstock.com.

Library of Congress Cataloging-in-Publication Data

Names: Lyman, Geraldine, author.
Title: Meteorology and forecasting the weather / Geraldine Lyman.
Description: New York : PowerKids Press, [2019] | Series: Spotlight on
    weather and natural disasters
Identifiers: LCCN 2018011262| ISBN 9781508169062 (library bound) | ISBN
    9781508169086 (pbk.) | ISBN 9781508169093 (6 pack)
Subjects: LCSH: Weather forecasting--Juvenile literature. |
    Meteorology--Juvenile literature.
Classification: LCC QC995.43 .H39 2018 | DDC 551.63--dc23
LC record available at https://lccn.loc.gov/2018011262

Manufactured in the United States of America

CPSIA Compliance Information: Batch #CS18PK For further information contact Rosen Publishing, New York, New York at 1-800-237-9932.

CONTENTS

CHAPTER ONE

WHY IS WEATHER IMPORTANT?

Have you ever made plans and then worried about what the weather might be during that time? Did you check a weather forecast? Weather forecasts show you what the weather might be like for the next few hours, the entire day, or the next few days.

Flights can be delayed or canceled due to weather. Even hot weather can prevent planes from flying safely, so weather forecasts are very important.

Many people depend on weather forecasts. Farmers need to know whether it will rain or if the temperature will drop below freezing. People who run airlines need to have very thorough weather reports to know what's safe for planes. People who run electricity companies have to prepare for storms and heat waves.

One of the most important things weather forecasts can do is let you know if the weather is going to be dangerous. This can help you prepare for whatever weather may be on its way to you.

CHAPTER TWO

THE HISTORY OF FORECASTING

People have tried to **predict** the weather for thousands of years. As early as 650 BC, the Babylonians used cloud patterns and astronomy to make predictions about the weather. By 300 BC, the Chinese created a weather calendar that split the year into 24 festivals, and each festival related to a different type of weather.

Meteorology wasn't very reliable, or trustworthy, until people invented several tools that helped them learn about the **atmosphere**. Once people created the thermometer in 1592 and invented the **barometer** in 1643, they started to observe and record weather on a regular basis. Observations led to reliable ideas about how weather forms and how it can be predicted.

As more people began using these tools, they'd share their observations and predict what would happen in one place by watching what was happening in another. This is still an important part of forecasting today.

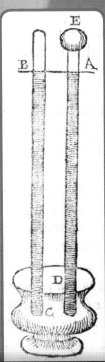

This drawing of an early barometer comes from *Lezioni Accademiche d'Evangelista Torricelli*, or *Academic Lessons of Evangelista Torricelli*. Torricelli is credited with the invention of the barometer.

CHAPTER THREE

WHO FORECASTS THE WEATHER?

Meteorologists are people who use science, math, and **technology** to study the atmosphere. Meteorologists do many different things. Some do **research**, learning about certain weather-related subjects such as clouds or wind patterns. These types of meteorologists are called atmospheric researchers. Others look at weather throughout history and how climate has changed. These people are called climatologists.

Meteorologists are most well known for forecasting the weather. They use their knowledge of the atmosphere to figure out what the weather will be like in a certain area. They often work in their communities to teach people how to prepare for different types of weather.

Climatologists used **satellites** to see where hot spots formed and caused land fires in Pekanbaru, Indonesia.

CHAPTER FOUR

FORECASTING METHODS

Today, meteorologists use four different forecasting methods to predict the weather:

1 Persistence forecasting: This type of forecasting predicts that the future weather will be the same as the current weather. Meteorologists create this forecast by observing with their eyes and ears and using special tools.

2 Synoptic forecasting: This type of forecasting looks at synoptic charts and broad patterns to predict the weather. A synoptic chart is any chart or map that presents data that describes the state of the atmosphere over a large area at a given moment in time.

3 Statistical forecasting: This type of forecasting uses past observed weather data to help predict the weather.

4 Computer forecasting: This type of forecasting uses computers to create weather models from observations, which provide meteorologists with a forecast for the next few days.

Sometimes meteorologists work together to combine these methods to create a more **accurate** weather forecast.

CHAPTER FIVE

WHAT'S IN A WEATHER FORECAST?

What does it take to create a weather forecast? If you check the weather on a phone, it might just tell you the temperature and if it's likely to rain. However, weather forecasts on TV or online will provide you with a lot more information.

When giving a forecast, meteorologists explain the symbols as the patterns move across the map.

A weather forecast may show a map of an area, large or small. Meteorologists will then use different **symbols** to show how the atmosphere above the mapped area may change over a period of time. These symbols stand for different parts of weather measured by a meteorologist. In a forecast, a map may show warm fronts and cold fronts, cloud cover, wind speed and direction, temperature, dew point, and **barometric pressure**. Sometimes a meteorologist will include more information, such as the heat index or wind chill.

CHAPTER SIX

LIGHTER THAN AIR

Did you know that air has weight? Air rises and falls and expands, or gets bigger, and contracts. Barometric pressure, another term for atmospheric pressure, is something meteorologists talk about a lot. Barometric pressure is usually talked about in terms of low-pressure and high-pressure systems.

Warm air spreads out more in a given space, which often means it has lower pressure and tends to rise. Cold air takes up less space, is heavier, and has higher pressure. It tends to sink.

Warm air and cold air have other properties, too, such as their ability to form clouds. Systems are constantly moving around and changing places with each other. The movement of high- and low-pressure systems is what we experience as weather. Meteorologists use barometers to keep track of these systems.

An aneroid barometer measures atmospheric pressure through a small metal box, called an aneroid cell, that expands and contracts depending on the pressure. Today, most people use electronic barometers.

CHAPTER SEVEN

CLOUDS AND PRECIPITATION

Precipitation is water that falls to the ground as hail, mist, rain, sleet, or snow. Depending on the barometric pressure in a certain area, meteorologists can make a guess at what kind of precipitation your area may experience.

When shelf clouds like this one form, you can practically see where the high-pressure and low-pressure systems meet.

High-pressure systems are usually associated with clear skies. Low-pressure systems can mean a storm is coming. This is because systems can hold different amounts of water vapor. Air in a high-pressure system holds lots of tiny gas **molecules** in a small space. Many of these molecules are water vapor. This means this vapor doesn't form clouds and the skies are clear.

However, if that air rises and spreads out, it releases water vapor. This vapor forms clouds, which create precipitation when they get too heavy!

CHAPTER EIGHT

WEATHERTECH

To get the most accurate forecast possible, meteorologists use cutting-edge technology. A special type of **radar** can detect precipitation levels, wind direction, wind speed, and warm fronts and cold fronts for a large area. That's a lot of information for a forecast!

Meteorologists can also use weather balloons to get information to help forecast the weather. Weather balloons filled with helium (a gas lighter than air) carry scientific instruments 24 miles (38.6 km) or higher into the atmosphere. When they hit the outer edge of the atmosphere, they pop. Then, the instruments fall down to Earth, collecting atmospheric readings.

Computer forecasting uses incredibly powerful computers called supercomputers. These supercomputers process data collected by weather balloons and create weather models. When making these models, the computers consider Earth's rotation, solar **radiation**, currents, the water cycle, and more.

Weather balloons are released every day all over the world. Without the information these instruments collect, we'd have a much harder time predicting the weather. The men in this picture are releasing a weather balloon at a weather station in the Arctic region around 1965.

CHAPTER NINE

GETTING THE WORD OUT

Another important part of forecasting is making sure the community knows what the weather has in store. Weather forecasters present their reports in newspapers, on television, and on the Internet.

To inform the public, meteorologists create forecast maps, graphs, and tables. They try to make **complex** information about the atmosphere easy to understand.

It takes a lot of practice to use a green screen. Imagine trying to point to something on the screen when there's actually nothing there.

NATIONAL WEATHER
WEATHER NEWS

COLD BLAST

Sometimes weather forecasters go to a place where a weather event is happening to present a live weather forecast. Other times, they stand in front of a green screen. This is a wall that is a bright green color. Computers place special images over everything green. So, if the meteorologist is wearing a green shirt, her green shirt will become part of the weather map. Meteorologists use green screens to show maps and graphics of the current and future weather.

CHAPTER TEN

AMAZING SCIENTISTS

Meteorologists are amazing scientists. They collect data and make predictions on what the weather will be like, all based on the current state of the atmosphere and other signs. Some dive into research, while others work hard to make sure their community is informed about the weather.

The next time you want to check the weather, try thinking about the tools meteorologists use. Then, make your own weather prediction. Even though you may not be able to use all the different types of forecasting, you can make your own persistence forecast by looking at the skies or reading a barometer. Once you have your data, guess what the weather will be like. Do you think there's a high-pressure or low-pressure system? Will the sky be clear or will there be clouds? Follow the weather and see if you're right. You might be a meteorologist in the making!

GLOSSARY

accurate (AA-kyuh-ruht) Free of mistakes.

atmosphere (AT-muh-sfeer) The whole mass of air that surrounds Earth.

barometer (buh-RAH-muh-tuhr) An instrument that measures air pressure and is used to forecast changes in the weather.

barometric pressure (behr-uh-MEH-trik PREH-shuhr) The pressure put forth in every direction at any given point by the weight of the atmosphere.

complex (KAHM-pleks) Not easy to understand or explain, having many parts.

meteorology (mee-tee-uh-RAH-luh-jee) A science that deals with the atmosphere, weather, and weather forecasting.

molecule (MAH-lih-kyool) The smallest possible amount of something that has all the characteristics of that thing.

predict (prih-DIKT) To guess what will happen in the future based on facts or knowledge.

radar (RAY-dahr) A device that sends out radio waves for finding out the position and speed of a moving object.

radiation (ray-dee-AY-shuhn) Energy that comes from a source in the form of waves or rays you can't see.

research (REE-suhrch) Careful study that is done to find and report new knowledge about something.

satellite (SAA-tuh-lyte) A spacecraft placed in orbit around Earth, a moon, or a planet to collect information or for communication.

symbol (SIM-buhl) Something, such as a picture or shape, that stands for something else.

technology (tek-NAH-luh-jee) A method that uses science to solve problems and the tools used to solve those problems.

INDEX

PRIMARY SOURCE LIST

Page 7
Diagram of an early barometer or measuring device. Woodcut. E. Torricelli. 1715. Now held at the Library of Congress Prints and Photographs Division, Washington, D.C.

Page 12
Forecast from the Afternoon Issuance of March 1, 2018. National Weather Service Weather Prediction Center.

Page 19
Weather Balloon. Photograph. ca. 1965. Fox Photos/Hulton Archive/Getty Images.

WEBSITES

Due to the changing nature of Internet links, PowerKids Press has developed an online list of websites related to the subject of this book. This site is updated regularly. Please use this link to access the list: www.powerkidslinks.com/swnd/meteor